THE SENSES

Words in *italics* in the main
text (*or in* Roman *type in
the captions*) are explained
in the Index and glossary at
the end of the book.

A Cherrytree Book

Adapted by A S Publishing
from COM FUNCIONEN ELS NOSTRES SENTITS
by Jaume Ripoll Metge
illustrated by Estudio Marcel Socías
© Parramón Ediciones, S.A. – 1992

This edition first published 1994
by Cherrytree Press Ltd
a subsidiary of
The Chivers Company Ltd
Windsor Bridge Road
Bath, Avon BA2 3AX

© Cherrytree Press Ltd 1994

British Library Cataloguing in Publication Data

The Senses
   I. Halton, Frances
   612.8

   ISBN 0-7451-5214-7

   Reprinted 1997

Typeset by Dorchester Typesetting, Dorset
Printed in Spain

INVISIBLE WORLD

THE
SENSES

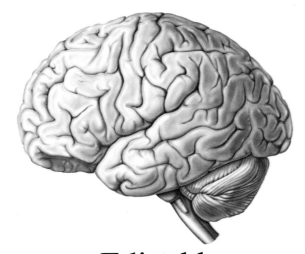

Edited by
Frances Halton

CHERRYTREE BOOKS

The sense organs

How do we find out what is happening all around us? We use our *external senses* – sight, hearing, touch, taste and smell. They give us information from our surroundings. Other *internal senses* tell us what is happening to our body. They tell us about the position of our limbs, whether our muscles are tired, whether we are hungry, thirsty or in pain, whether our bladder is full and so on.

All the information from our internal and external senses is analysed in our *brain*, and then we respond to it. Without information supplied by our senses we could not function properly or safely. Some people lack one or more of the senses. Often they manage very well, but life is considerably more difficult for them, and many pleasures are lost to them.

Our bodies contain sense organs with *receptor cells* that respond to certain physical or chemical *stimuli* such as light, sound and smells. The receptors are quite different from one another, and each kind reacts only to a specific type of stimulus. The stimuli are turned into nervous impulses that are sent along a network of *nerves* that link the sense organs to the brain.

The brain – which acts as the central computer of our body – converts each type of information into *sensations* that we become aware of and prompts us to respond. When the doorbell rings, signals go from our ears to the brain. The brain interprets the sound and sends nerve signals to the muscles to make us move and answer the door. We consciously respond to sensations, such as the ring of the doorbell. But in some cases our responses are unthinking *reflex actions*, originating not in the brain but in the nerves of the *spinal cord*.

The brain, seen sliced through, from above. Different sense centres are found in different areas.

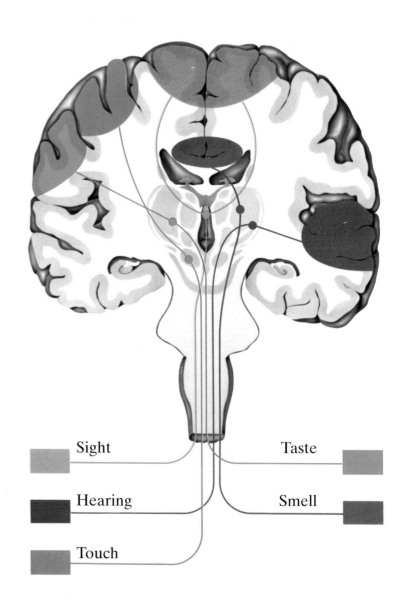

Sight

Hearing

Touch

Taste

Smell

THE EXTERNAL SENSES			
Sense	**Organ**	**Sensitive cells**	**Stimulus**
Sight	eye	*cones* and *rods*	light
Hearing	ear	*organ of Corti*	sound waves
Taste	tongue	*taste buds*	chemical contact
Smell	nose	*olfactory cells*	chemical contact
Touch	skin	*tactile corpuscles*	physical contact

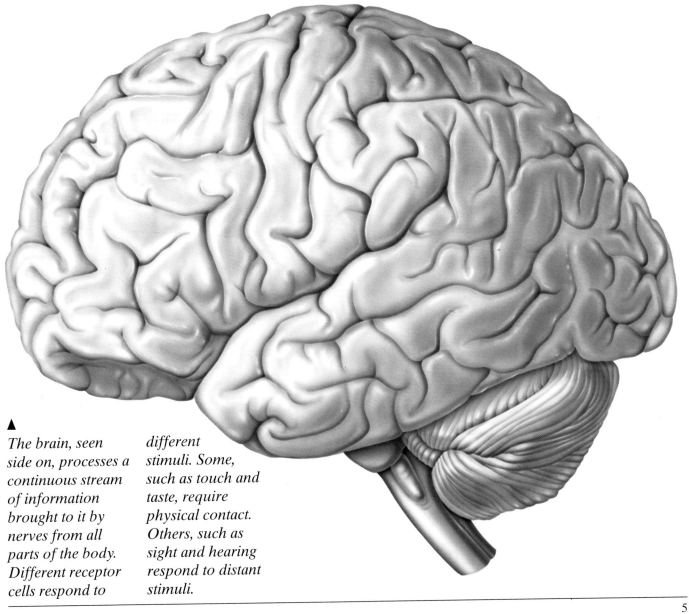

▲
The brain, seen side on, processes a continuous stream of information brought to it by nerves from all parts of the body. Different receptor cells respond to different stimuli. Some, such as touch and taste, require physical contact. Others, such as sight and hearing respond to distant stimuli.

Sight

Sight is the most important of all our senses. The part of the brain dealing with sight is much larger than the areas dealing with our other senses.

Our eyes are our organs of sight. They are spherical in shape, and are located in the orbits, or eye sockets. Each eye socket is surrounded by the bones of the skull; it contains the eyeball and structures related to it, including muscles, glands and coverings. These move and protect the eye, and help to keep it in the best possible condition.

The bony eye socket protects most of the surface of the eye, except for the front. This is protected by the eyelids, which can close over the eye.

The eyelids are lined by a membrane called the *conjunctiva* which extends down over the front of the eyeball. It produces *mucus*, a clear shiny fluid that lubricates the eyeball. The eyelids protect the eyes from flying dust, wind, scratches and other contacts. They also help to control the amount of light that enters the eye. In a bright light, for example, we often 'screw up our eyes', partly closing our eyelids against the glare. From the edge of each eyelid grow tiny hairs called eyelashes, which catch dust particles.

Above the eye sockets are the eyebrows. These divert drops of rain or sweat running down the forehead to

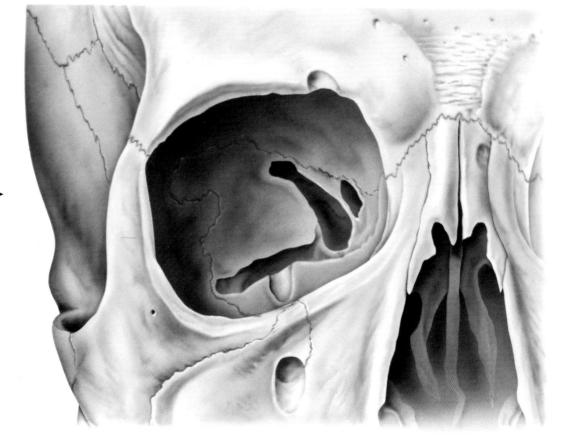

Each eye socket is ▶ *a space surrounded by the bones of the skull, which form a hard case that holds and protects the eyeball. The opening at the back of the socket allows the* optic nerve *to pass through to the brain.*

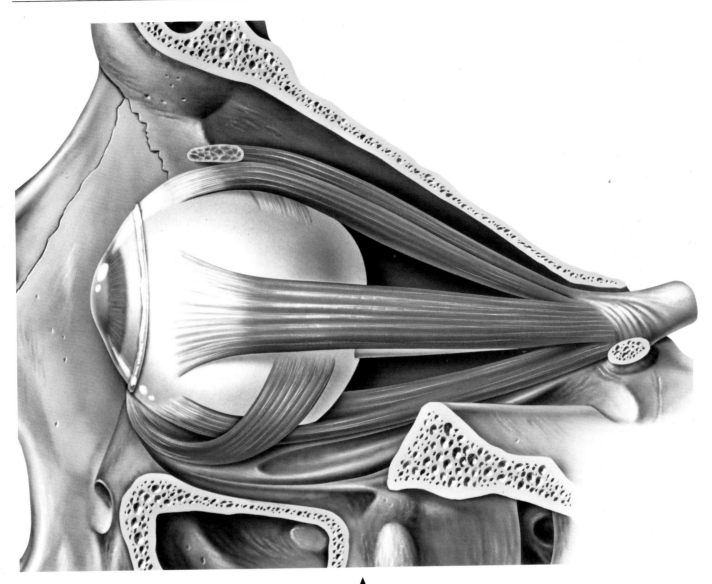

the outside of the face, so that they do not fall into the eyes.

Around the eyes are *tear glands*, which produce a fluid that keeps the eyeball moist and clean, and washes away dust and other 'foreign bodies'.

The eyeballs are held in position by muscles that control their movement. Normally both eyes move and work together as a single unit, co-ordinated by the brain.

▲
The bones (1) of the skull provide a safe cavity for the eyeball. Attached to the eyeball are six muscles (2) that enable it to rotate within the socket. The muscles meet at a fibrous ring at the back of the eye (3).

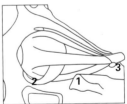

The eye

The walls of the eyeball are made up of three layers of *tissue*: the *sclera*, the *choroid* and the *retina*. The sclera forms the visible 'white' of the eye. At the front of the eye the sclera gives way to a transparent bulge called the *cornea*. This is the 'window' of the eye through which light enters.

The second layer, the choroid, contains many blood vessels. At the front of the eye it forms a circular area of muscles, called the *iris*. This is the coloured part of the eye which surrounds the black-looking opening called the *pupil*. The iris opens and closes to control the amount of light entering the eye through the pupil.

Immediately behind the iris is the *lens*, a flexible, crystal-clear structure, about the size and shape of a headache pill. Muscles in the choroid alter the shape of the lens to focus images on the retina. This layer lines the back part of the eyeball. It contains light-sensitive nerve cells, which transmit messages through the optic nerve to the brain.

The space between the cornea and the iris is called the front chamber. It is filled with a watery fluid called the *aqueous humour*. The space between the lens and the retina is called the back chamber. It contains a thicker but equally transparent fluid called the *vitreous* humour. Vitreous means glassy.

The membranes of ▶ the eye. The sclera is the tough, outermost layer of the eye. At the front of the eye is the transparent cornea. The middle layer of the eye is called the choroid. It contains muscles and the blood vessels that supply the interior of the eye. The retina is the innermost layer of the eyeball. It contains the sense cells that are stimulated by the light.

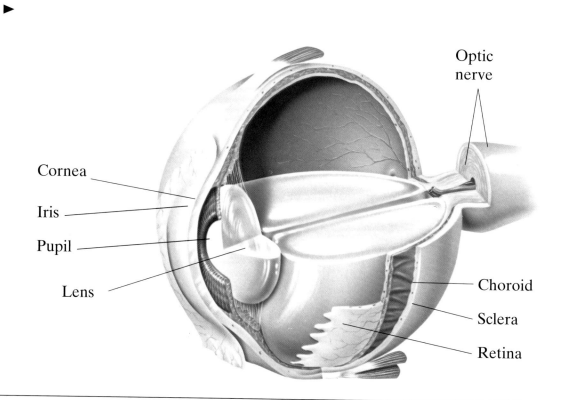

Optic nerve

Cornea

Iris

Pupil

Lens

Choroid

Sclera

Retina

Different parts of the retina (**1**) carry out different functions. The yellow spot *area* (**2**) *is the area of maximum vision.*

▼

The point where the optic nerve leaves the eye (**3**) is a small blind spot where there are no light-sensitive cells. We do not notice it

because of the continuous movement of our eyes. The cornea (**4**) and the lens (**6**) enclose the front chamber which is

filled with a fluid called the aqueous humour. The back chamber (**5**) is filled with a fluid called the vitreous humour.

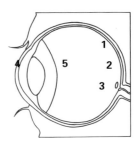

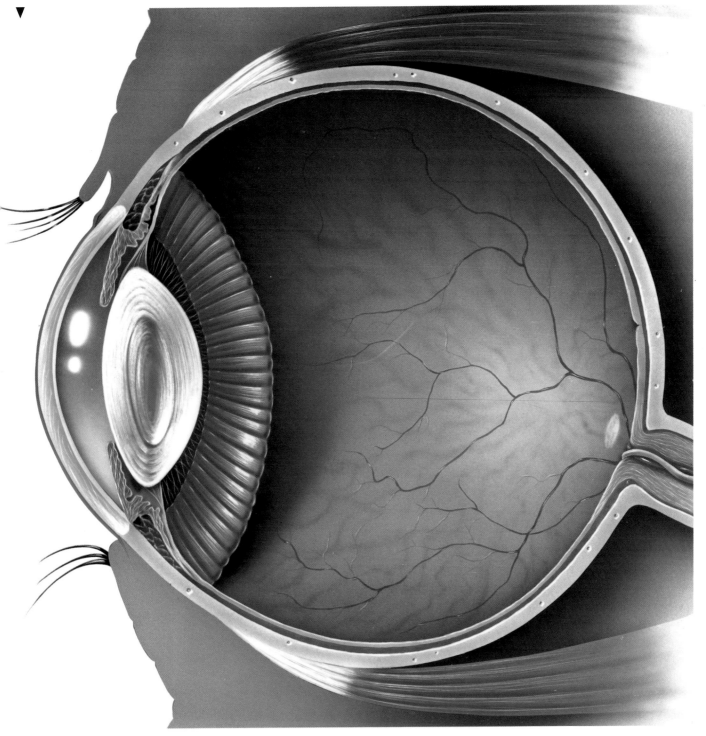

How we see

Light reflected off objects enters the eye through the curved cornea, and passes through the pupil to the lens. The lens bulges or flattens to bend the light rays to a *focus* on the retina. The rays of light form a small inverted image on the light-sensitive cells. It is not a true image but a mass of nerve impulses that the brain interprets as a 'picture' for us to see.

The cells of the retina are called rods and cones because of their shape. There are many more rods than cones – about 125 million rods and only seven million cones. The rods are very sensitive to light and enable us to see when the light is dim, but they cannot distinguish colours. The cones are sensitive to colour and fine detail. They are found mainly in the *fovea*, the central part of an area called the yellow spot, which is the point of maximum vision. The cones do not work in poor light, which is why everything looks grey or black at dusk. Nerve fibres link the rods and cones to the optic nerve, which carries information from the retina to the optic centre of the brain.

Some people do not see very clearly. A person who cannot see distant objects is said to be short sighted. The reason for this is that the eye is too long from front to back, and the image of a distant object is not in focus on the retina. If the eye is too short, distant objects are clear but nearby ones are blurred; the person is long sighted. These problems can be overcome by wearing spectacles or contact lenses to focus the images correctly.

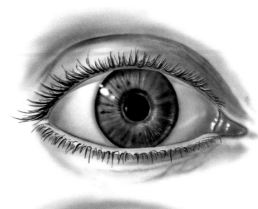

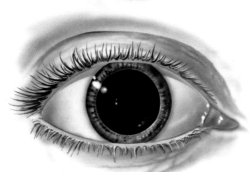

◀ *The amount of light that enters the eye is controlled by the iris. In dim light (bottom) its muscles make the pupil dilate (enlarge); in bright light (top) they reduce its size. A substance called* melanin *gives the iris its colour.*

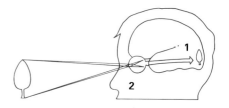

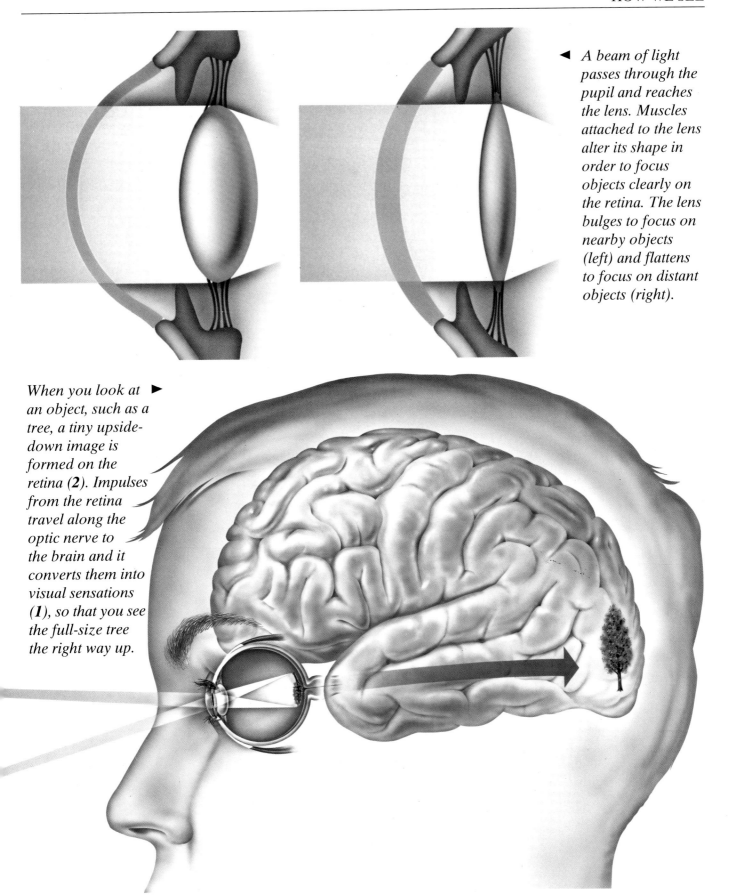

◄ *A beam of light passes through the pupil and reaches the lens. Muscles attached to the lens alter its shape in order to focus objects clearly on the retina. The lens bulges to focus on nearby objects (left) and flattens to focus on distant objects (right).*

When you look at ► an object, such as a tree, a tiny upside-down image is formed on the retina (2). Impulses from the retina travel along the optic nerve to the brain and it converts them into visual sensations (1), so that you see the full-size tree the right way up.

The ear

Sounds are vibrations in the air. They move through the air in invisible waves, spreading like the ripples in a pond when you throw a stone in. Our hearing is so sensitive that we can translate these vibrations into all sorts of different sounds.

Most of the working parts of the ear are buried deep inside the skull. Each ear has three distinct regions: the *outer ear*, the *middle ear*, and the *inner ear*.

The outer ear consists of the ear flap and the *ear passage*, the first part of the *auditory canal*. The ear flap – the visible part that we usually call the ear – is made of flexible *cartilage*, and it acts as a funnel to gather sounds from the surroundings. The sounds travel along the auditory canal for about 20 millimetres to the *eardrum*, a membrane stretched across the passage. The sound vibrations make it vibrate.

The auditory canal is lined with skin that has small hairs in it and special sweat glands that produce wax. Together the hairs and wax protect the eardrum by trapping dust particles and keeping water out. Sometimes a build-up of wax in the ear has to be removed by the doctor. Never try to remove wax yourself or poke objects into your ear. You could damage your eardrum.

The eardrum separates the outer ear from the middle ear. This is inside the skull, and contains three tiny linked bones called *ossicles*. They are the smallest bones in the body and get their names – *hammer, anvil,* and *stirrup* – from their shapes. The bones pick up the vibrations of the eardrum and transmit them to the membrane that covers the *oval window*, leading to the inner ear. The inner ear contains receptor cells that are sensitive to the sound vibrations. It also contains the organs that give us our sense of balance.

A narrow tube called the *eustachian tube* connects the middle ear to the back of the throat. Mostly the tube is closed, but it opens when you swallow, yawn, blow your nose or open your mouth. This allows air to pass into the middle ear and make the pressure on the inner side of the eardrum equal to that on the outside.

The ear flap is the only part of our hearing system that lies outside the body. It leads directly to the auditory canal inside the skull.
▼

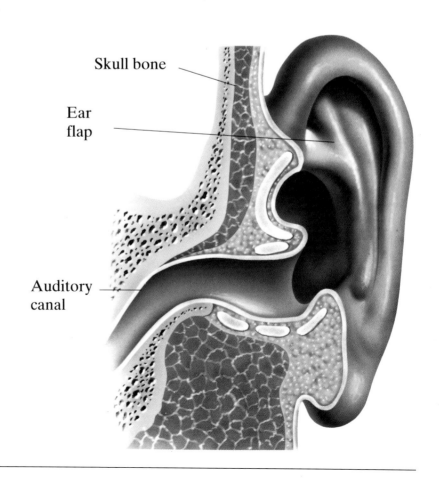

Skull bone

Ear flap

Auditory canal

The chain of three ► tiny movable bones - the hammer, anvil and stirrup - which pass sound vibrations from the eardrum to the inner ear.

The eardrum (**1**) passes vibrations to the chain of ossicle bones (**2**) to which it is connected. The eustachian tube (**3**) leads to the throat and makes sure that the air pressure in the middle ear is the same as that on the outside. If the pressure were unequal, the eardrum might be damaged by sudden changes in pressure. The oval window (**4**) marks the beginning of the inner ear. ▼

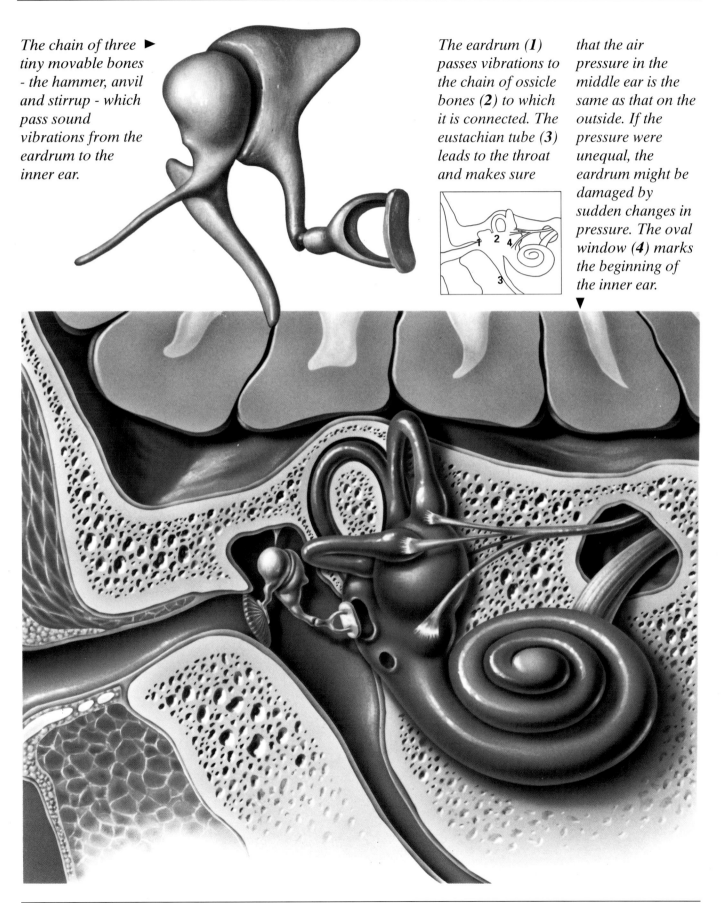

The inner ear

The inner ear starts at the oval window. It is made up of a series of fluid-filled chambers and tunnels known as the *labyrinth* (a labyrinth is another name for a maze). The main parts of the labyrinth are the *semicircular canals* and the *cochlea*. The semicircular canals are concerned with balance, the cochlea with hearing.

The cochlea is the innermost part of the ear. It is a spirally-coiled fluid-filled tube that looks like a snail shell. It is lined with a delicate membrane that contains thousands of hairlike receptor cells, collectively known as the organ of Corti. This is the actual organ of hearing. The hair cells lie right inside the cochlea, and are moved by any movement of the fluid. The hair cells convert vibrations in the fluid into nerve impulses and relay them along the *auditory nerve* to the brain, which interprets them as sounds we can hear.

The inner ear consists of fluid-filled canals and chambers. Vibration of the oval window sets the cochlear fluid in motion, and the round window moves in and out to take up the pressure. Inside the coils of the cochlea (cut through, left) are the minute receptor cells that make up the organ of Corti.
▼

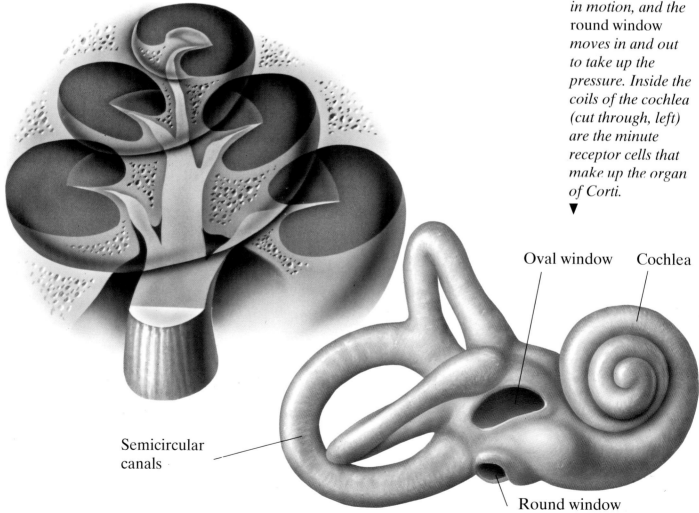

Oval window   Cochlea

Semicircular canals

Round window

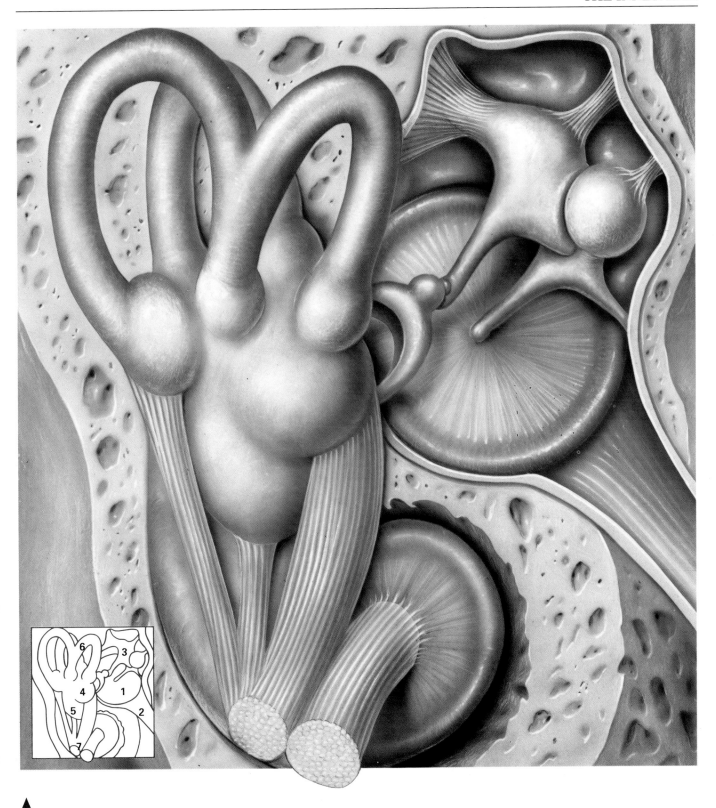

▲
This cross-section of the ear shows how its different parts are connected. We can see the eardrum (**1**), the eustachian tube (**2**), the tiny bones of the middle ear (**3**), the utricle (**4**) and the saccule (**5**), the semicircular canals (**6**) and the nerve endings that carry to the brain the impulses that become the sensation of hearing (**7**). These nerves also send information to the brain concerning our balance.

How we hear

A source of sound generates waves in the air. These are captured by the ear flap. The flap is specially shaped so that it catches the sound waves and directs them towards the auditory canal. Human beings cannot move their ear flaps but dogs and other mammals can 'prick' their ears to make sure no sound escapes them.

The waves pass along the auditory canal to the eardrum, which begins to vibrate. The vibrations of the eardrum are transmitted and amplified (made stronger) by the chain of ossicles. The movement of the stirrup bone against the oval window at the start of the inner ear causes it to vibrate. The vibrations of the oval window are transmitted through the fluid in the inner ear in the form of waves. Inside the spiral cochlea the receptor cells of the organ of Corti are moved by the moving fluid. The cells are connected to nerve fibres which convert the movements into nerve impulses that are carried by the auditory nerve to the brain.

The receptor cells in different parts of the cochlea are sensitive to sounds of different *frequency* or *pitch*, and the brain interprets the signals from these different areas as different sounds. The loudness of a sound depends on the number of receptor cells that send impulses to the brain. The stronger the sound wave, the more receptor cells will be moved.

We know the direction from which a sound comes because we have two ears. A fractional difference in the time it takes for a sound to reach each ear is recognized by the brain and enables us to sense the direction.

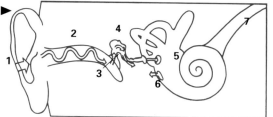

We hear when a sound wave (1) passes through the auditory canal (2) and strikes the eardrum (3), making the ossicles vibrate (4). These bones transmit the vibrations to the oval window (5) which sets the fluid of the cochlea in motion. The flow of the liquid moves the receptor cells of the organ of Corti, generating nervous impulses which are transmitted along the auditory nerve (7). The movement also causes the round window (6) to bulge in and out to maintain equal pressure inside and outside the inner ear.

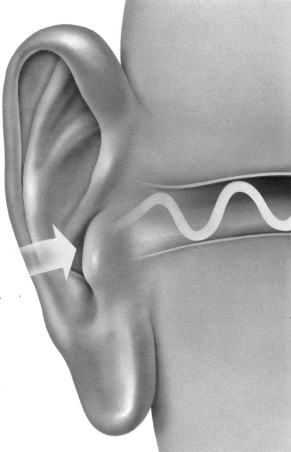

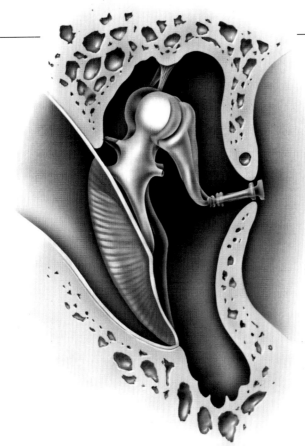

◄ *The ossicles act like levers, passing on movement. Because the oval window is so much smaller than the eardrum, vibrations against it are much more powerful. This is useful because the vibrations do not travel as easily through the cochlear fluid as through the air or solid bones.*

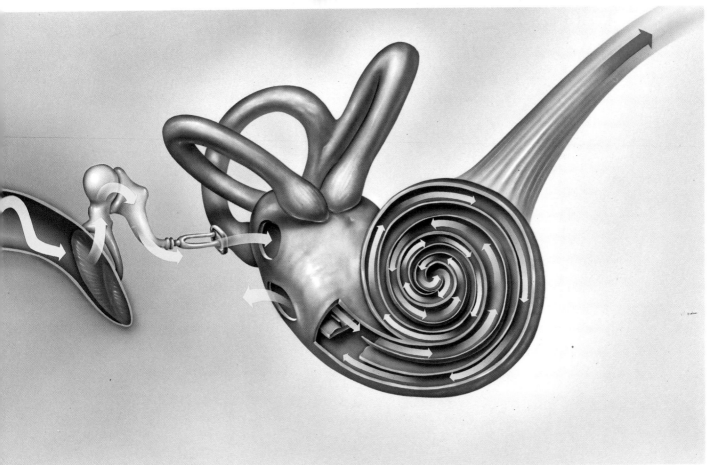

Balance

Our sense of balance is important because it tells us about the position of our body in relation to its surroundings, and of any changes in this position. Without it, we would find it difficult to stand upright or move around. The mechanisms of the sense of balance are located in the inner ear. They consist of the semicircular canals and two adjoining pouches called the utricle and saccule.

Each of the semicircular canals is in a different plane. Two are vertical and at right angles to each other. One is horizontal. Each widens out at the end into an area called the *ampulla*, and is connected with the utricule and saccule. Like the cochlea, these channels and chambers are filled with fluid and contain hair-like receptor cells connected to nerve fibres. In the ampullae the hairs project into jelly-like material. Movement of the head causes the fluid inside the semicircular canals to move. As it moves the fluid stimulates the receptor cells in different parts of the canals. If it flows one way in one canal it will flow the opposite way in another. It will stimulate more receptors in one, and fewer in the other. Impulses from the receptor cells travel to the brain along the auditory nerve. By comparing the different impulses from the six canals (three in each ear), the brain can calculate the direction of any movement.

Inside the utricle and saccule there are tiny solid particles of a stony material that brush against the receptor cells and stimulate them. These little stones, called otoliths, respond to gravity. From their movement, the brain can tell the position of the head at any time.

When we make a sudden movement, the message may not get to the brain quickly enough, and so we 'lose our balance' and fall. When we spin round several times and then stop, the fluid in the canals continues to move for a little while – telling the brain that we are still moving. The brain is confused, and we feel dizzy for a short time until the fluid stops moving.

The semicircular canals are set at right angles to one another, like these semicircles drawn on card. When you move your head in any direction, the fluid in all the canals moves, stimulating nerves in some parts of the canals more than others. With information coming from two ears, the brain is aware of every movement.

▼

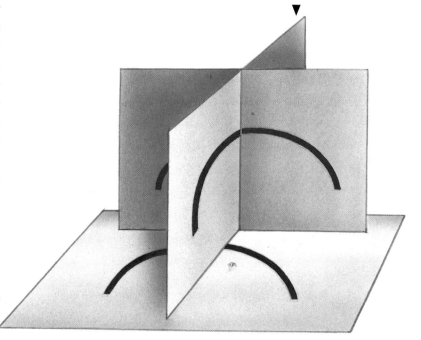

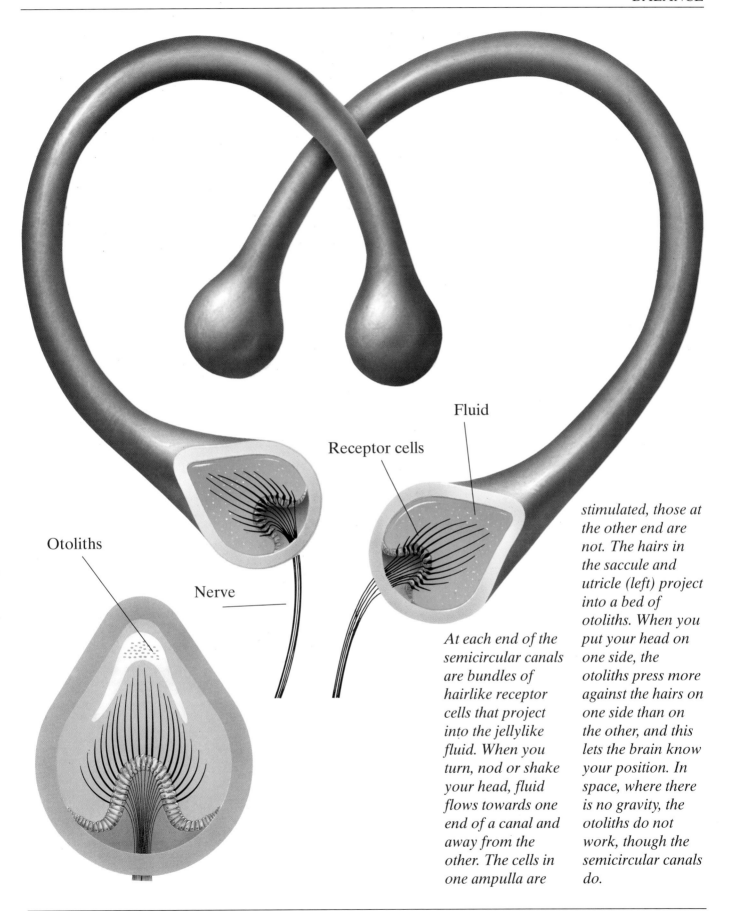

Fluid

Receptor cells

Otoliths

Nerve

At each end of the semicircular canals are bundles of hairlike receptor cells that project into the jellylike fluid. When you turn, nod or shake your head, fluid flows towards one end of a canal and away from the other. The cells in one ampulla are stimulated, those at the other end are not. The hairs in the saccule and utricle (left) project into a bed of otoliths. When you put your head on one side, the otoliths press more against the hairs on one side than on the other, and this lets the brain know your position. In space, where there is no gravity, the otoliths do not work, though the semicircular canals do.

Smell

When we smell something, we are recognizing tiny traces of chemicals that have been released into the air by a particular substance. Humans do not have a very well-developed sense of smell compared with other mammals. If you watch a dog, you will see that it is noticing all sorts of different smells that you cannot detect at all.

The receptor cells that detect smells are called *olfactory cells*. They are deep inside the nose. The nose is divided vertically by a wall of cartilage into two nostrils through which air passes when we breathe. The nostrils lead to two *nasal passages* (each divided by three shelf-like bones called turbinates). Breathed-in air is drawn through the nasal passages to the back of the throat and down the *windpipe* to the *lungs*.

The nostrils and nasal passages are lined with a soft mucous membrane covered with tiny hairs called *cilia*.

The mucus and hairs trap dust, germs and liquid and move them to the back of the throat to be swallowed into the *digestive tract*, not inhaled into the lungs.

The turbinates and their mucous membrane also makes the air we breathe in moist and warm before it passes down to our lungs. One small part of the membrane in the upper part of the *nasal cavity* contains the olfactory cells that detect chemicals in the breathed-in air. These nerve receptors take nerve impulses to an area called the *olfactory bulb* behind the nasal cavity. From there the signals go into the brain where they are translated into smells that we can recognise.

Humans can tell the difference between over 3000 different chemicals. Smells can attract us or repel us. Most nutritious substances smell good, most poisons smell foul.

The nasal cavity is formed by the bones of the nose (1) and the skull (3). Air passes over the three layers of bone (2) called turbinates to the receptor cells at the back of the passage that leads to the olfactory bulb (4). ▶

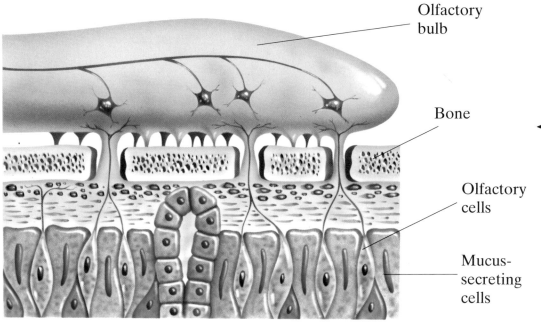

Olfactory bulb

Bone

Olfactory cells

Mucus-secreting cells

◀ *The olfactory cells are stimulated by chemicals in breathed-in air. Nerve fibres from the receptors link up inside the olfactory bulb, and carry their signals to the olfactory centre in the brain.*

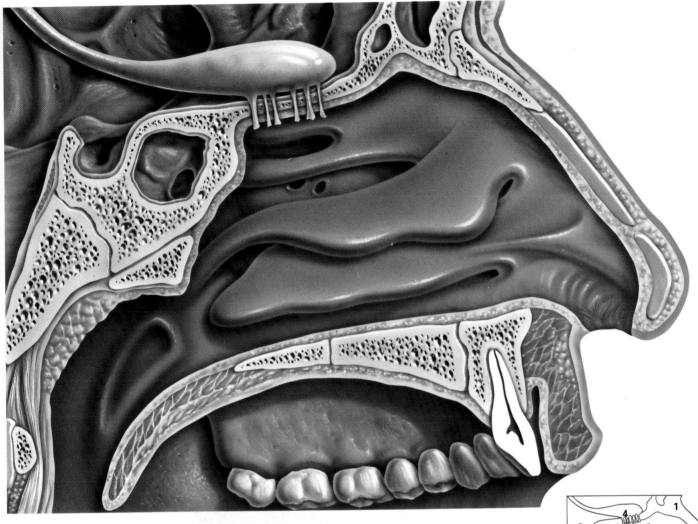

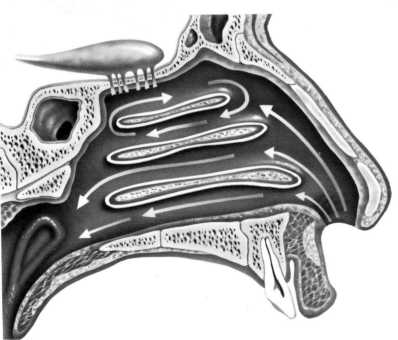

Air is warmed and ▶
filtered as it passes
over the turbinate
bones in the nose.
As it passes the
sense cells, we
recognize smells. If
the air smells bad we
might move quickly
away from the
source of the smell.
If it smells good, we
might sniff to bring
more of the air into
contact with the
sense cells.

Taste

Taste is another sense that relies on contact with chemicals, but when we taste food the flavour we recognize is a combination of taste and smell. The receptor cells for taste lie in the tongue. As we chew our food, sense receptors from the nose and tongue pass information to the brain.

The tongue consists mainly of muscular tissue and is completely covered by a mucous membrane. Your tongue feels fairly smooth inside your mouth, but if you look at it closely you will see that its surface is deeply fissured. Numerous little projections of a variety of shapes, called *papillae*, give it a rough, bumpy texture. The papillae and the sides of the fissures carry huge numbers of *taste buds*, which are clusters of sensitive receptor cells sunk into the mucous membrane.

Nerve impulses from the sensory cells in the taste buds travel along two nerves to the brain. One nerve carries tastes from the front of the tongue, the other from the back and sides, from about half way back. The nerve impulses go to a taste centre deep inside the brain that translates them into tastes that we can recognize.

The taste buds enable us to distinguish four primary tastes: sourness, bitterness, sweetness and saltiness. Each of these four main tastes is detected by a particular kind of receptor, located on a particular part of the tongue. Food must be moist to be tasted. If tongue and food are dry, there is no taste. Only when food begins to be dissolved by *saliva* can the taste buds work.

The flavour of our food comes from the mixture of the four basic tastes and our sense of smell. When you eat a good meal the taste of the food is preceded by the smell, and mixes with it. If you have a blocked nose and lose your sense of smell, you will find that your food loses almost all its flavour and you will recognize only the four basic tastes.

Salty and sweet tastes are most easily detected on the tip of the tongue. The buds that are sensitive to sourness are concentrated at the sides of the tongue. Bitter substances are detected by taste buds situated at the back of the tongue.
▼

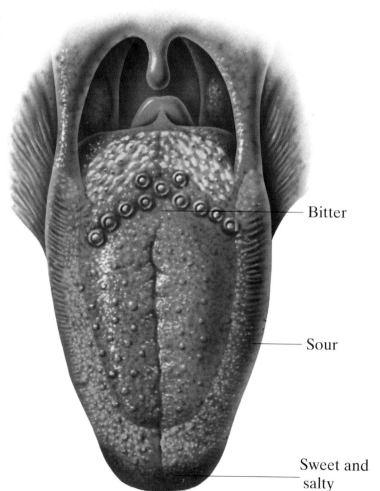

Bitter

Sour

Sweet and salty

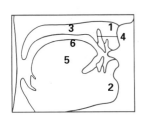

The tongue lies in the mouth, which is a space surrounded by the bones of the face – the upper jaw (**1**), lower jaw (**2**) and palate (**3**) – and by the teeth (**4**). The tongue consists of two main elements: a muscular part (**5**) which gives it strength and movement, and a mucous membrane (**6**) containing the taste buds.

▼

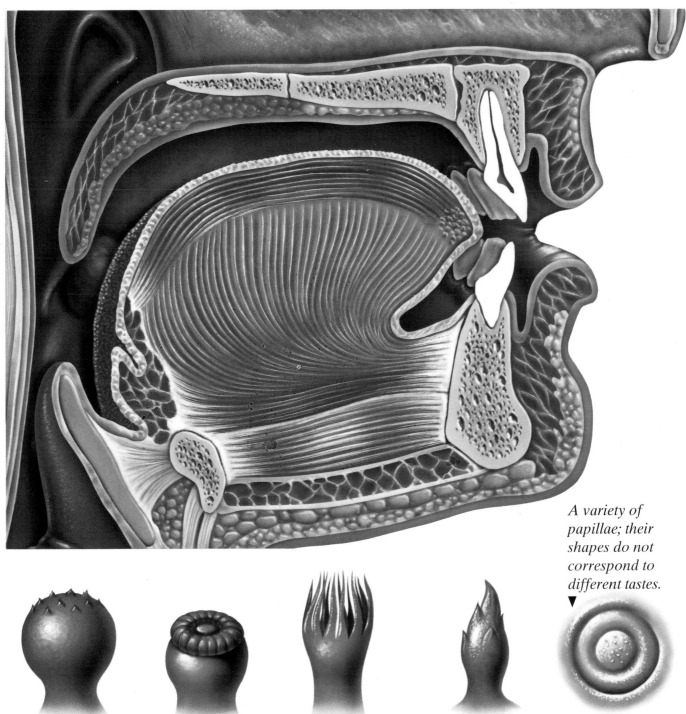

A variety of papillae; their shapes do not correspond to different tastes.

▼

The skin

Virtually every part of our body is sensitive to touch. Our senses of sight, hearing, smell and taste are precise. They each make us aware of a particular aspect of our surroundings. The sense of touch is less distinct. It makes us aware of contact, heat, cold, pressure and pain, and of sensations outside and inside our body.

Some parts of our body are far more sensitive to touch than others. Our fingertips, for instance, are extremely sensitive. People who are blind are able to 'read' through their fingertips, using an alphabet of raised dots called Braille.

The organ of touch is the skin. Skin covers all of the body. It provides us with a water-resistant, well-oiled covering that protects the interior of the body from conditions outside. It also helps to regulate our temperature (by sweating).

The skin is made up of three layers, the *epidermis*, the *dermis* and the *hypodermis*. The epidermis, the outermost layer of the skin, is a protective layer. It varies in thickness according to the amount of wear it gets. It is particularly thick on the soles of the feet and on the palms of the hand. The hypodermis is the skin's deepest layer. It is rich in the fatty tissue that helps to keep us warm.

Between these two layers is the dermis. This middle layer contains sweat and sebaceous (oil) glands, hair follicles, blood vessels, nerves and the special receptors involved in the sense of touch.

Our fingertips are extremely sensitive to touch and we use them so much that without our nails they might be damaged. Our nails are also useful tools that we use for delicate jobs. They are made of keratin, a tough, flexible material formed from hardened dead skin cells that is not sensitive to pain. If it were, we could not cut (or bite) our nails ▶

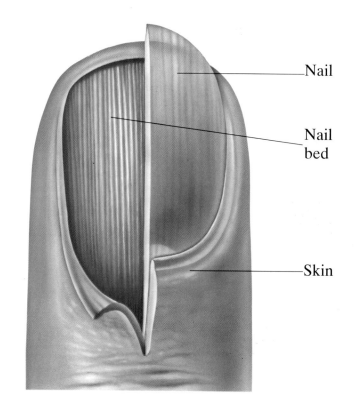

Nail

Nail bed

Skin

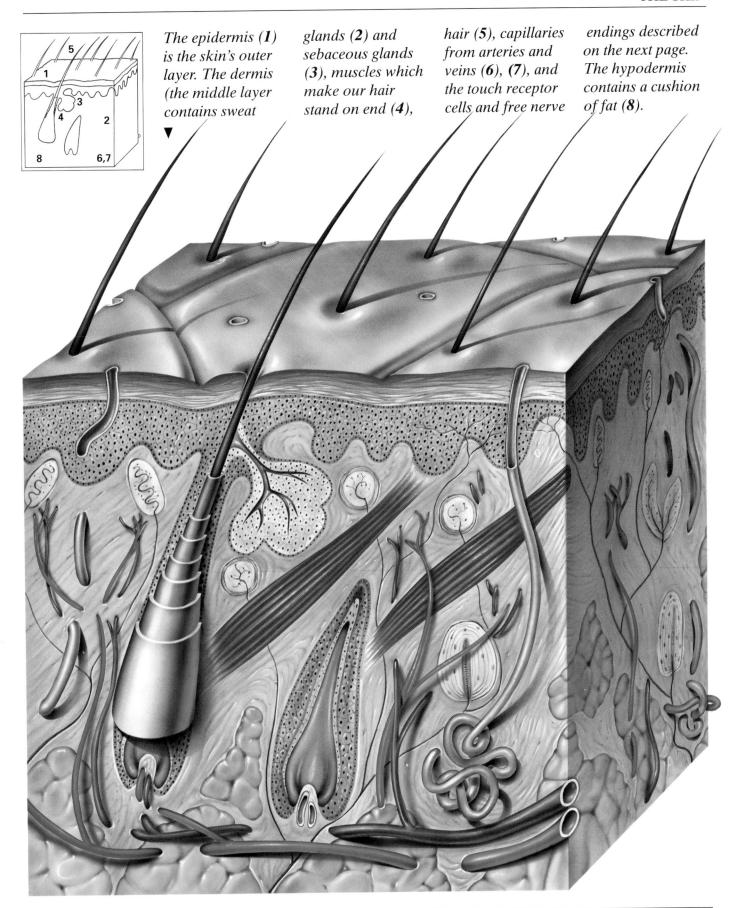

The epidermis (**1**) is the skin's outer layer. The dermis (the middle layer contains sweat glands (**2**) and sebaceous glands (**3**), muscles which make our hair stand on end (**4**), hair (**5**), capillaries from arteries and veins (**6**), (**7**), and the touch receptor cells and free nerve endings described on the next page. The hypodermis contains a cushion of fat (**8**).

▼

Touch and pain

The nerve receptors in the skin respond to contact (light touch), continuous pressure, heat and cold, and pain. There are two main types of receptors: tactile corpuscles and *free nerve endings*. Different types of tactile corpuscles deal with different sensations.

Meissner corpuscles, which lie near the surface of the skin, respond to contact. The sensitivity of an area depends on their distribution. There are more than a thousand in each fingertip, but few on the back of the hand.

Pacini corpuscles are located more deeply in the dermis, almost at the level of the hypodermis. They respond to pressure.

Ruffini corpuscles are heat receptors; *Krause corpuscles* cold receptors.

Free nerve endings in the skin and in internal organs are responsible for pain. All the receptors may be stimulated at the same time. For example, when someone shakes your hand, the receptors for contact, pressure and heat (or cold) are stimulated. If the shake turns into a squeeze, the pain receptors are also stimulated.

The sensation of pain is vital for our safety. It alerts us to danger and tells us when something is wrong inside us. If a danger is acute the body may react even before the brain is aware of the danger. The reflex action of jumping away from a sharp object or something hot may stop us being cut or burned. It is only after we have jumped away that we become aware of our action.

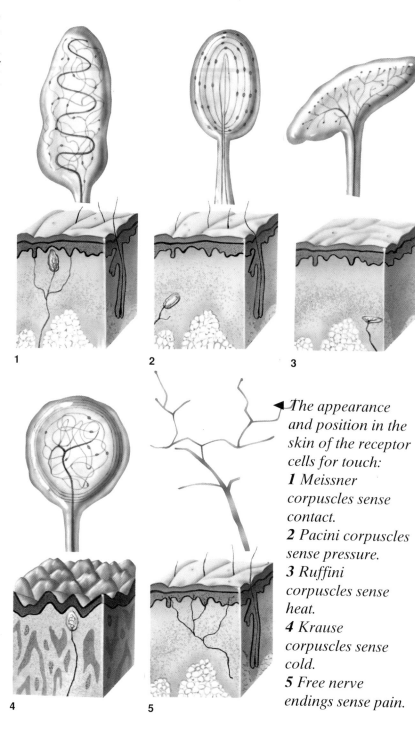

The appearance and position in the skin of the receptor cells for touch:
1 Meissner corpuscles sense contact.
2 Pacini corpuscles sense pressure.
3 Ruffini corpuscles sense heat.
4 Krause corpuscles sense cold.
5 Free nerve endings sense pain.

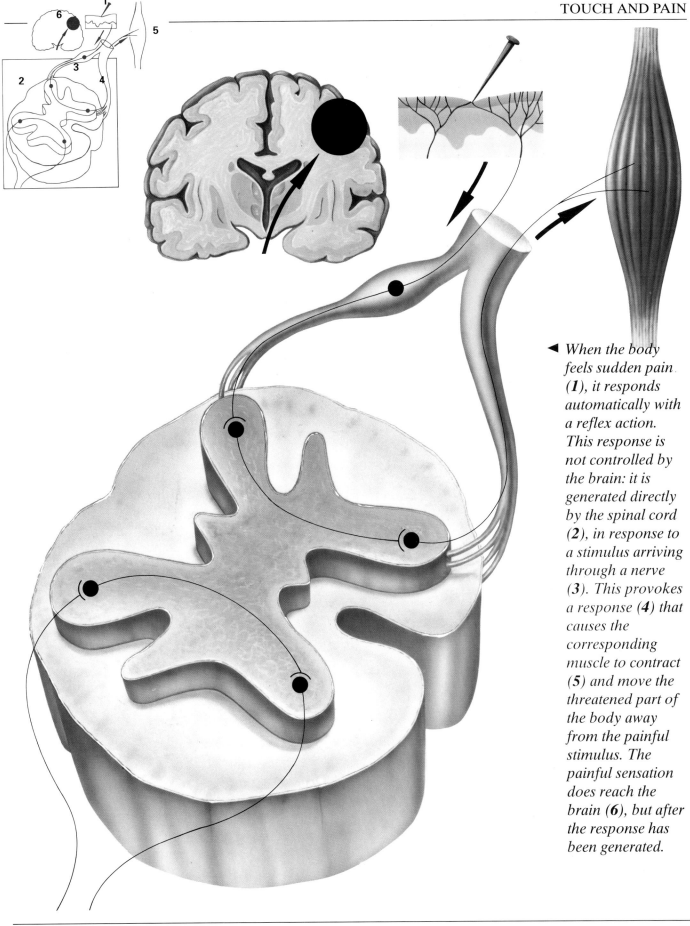

When the body feels sudden pain (**1**), it responds automatically with a reflex action. This response is not controlled by the brain: it is generated directly by the spinal cord (**2**), in response to a stimulus arriving through a nerve (**3**). This provokes a response (**4**) that causes the corresponding muscle to contract (**5**) and move the threatened part of the body away from the painful stimulus. The painful sensation does reach the brain (**6**), but after the response has been generated.

Finding out

Two into one

This experiment demonstrates that, although our two eyes see separately, our brain presents us with a single, unified image.

Draw a bird and a cage on two pieces of paper about the size of this page. Separate the two pictures by an upright piece of card. Now rest your nose on the cardboard, so that each eye can see only one drawing. Gaze at the pictures and in a very little while you will find that the picture your brain sends is that of the bird inside the cage. The brain has joined the two images together into one.

At your fingertips

Cut out pieces of smooth and rough materials – fabric, paper, cork, sandpaper and so on and stick them on to cardboard. Scatter them on a table top and, with your eyes closed, try to recognize the different textures. Ordinarily, we rely a great deal on our sight in recognizing substances. This game shows how sensitive our fingertips are, and helps develop the sense of touch. People who are blind have to rely greatly on their sense of touch. They become more sensitive than sighted people as a result.

Now you hear it, now you don't . . .

Hold a clock or watch with a quiet tick (or a radio with the volume turned low) near your ear and listen to the sound. Slowly move it away from your ear, until you cannot hear

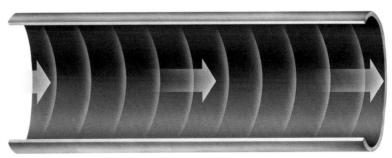

it. Measure how far away from your ear you are holding it.

Now make a tube out of paper or cardboard, about as long as the distance between the watch and your ear. Ask someone to hold the tube between your ear and the clock. You should hear the tick more clearly now. This is because the sound waves caused by the ticking normally spread out through the air. Enclosed in a tube, the waves travel in one direction only, just as sound waves do in your ear.

Taste and tell

The four basic tastes which the taste buds on the tongue can recognize are saltiness, sweetness, sourness and bitterness. Find food substances that have these tastes – table salt, sugar, lemon juice and coffee, for example. Think about your sensations as you taste them. Put small amounts of them on different areas of your tongue. Is the taste identical in all parts? Now shut your eyes and ask someone else to put a little of each substance on your tongue. How easily can you tell the different tastes apart?

Index and glossary